FULL-COLOR FLORAL DESIGNS IN THE ART NOUVEAU STYLE

By E. A. Seguy

Edited by Charles Rahn Fry

Dover Publications, Inc., New York

TO VIRGINIA FRY WESTON
GREENVILLE, OHIO

Copyright © 1977 by Dover Publications, Inc.
All rights reserved under Pan American and International
Copyright Conventions.

Published in Canada by General Publishing Company,
Ltd., 30 Lesmill Road, Don Mills, Toronto, Ontario.
Published in the United Kingdom by Constable and
Company, Ltd., 10 Orange Street, London WC2H 7EG.

This Dover edition, first published in 1977, contains 40
plates from the work *Les fleurs et leurs applications*

décoratives, originally published in two portfolios by the
Librairie des Arts Décoratifs (A. Calavas), Paris, n.d.
[1901]. See Introduction for further bibliographic details.

International Standard Book Number: 0-486-23439-8
Library of Congress Catalog Card Number: 76-45988

Manufactured in the United States of America
Dover Publications, Inc.
180 Varick Street
New York, N.Y. 10014

Introduction

Around 1900 in Paris it was the fashion to stylize the flower and incorporate it into decorative motifs. Floral designs were often influenced by Oriental forms such as waving, curling lines and soft, rounded shapes. Following the philosophical tenets of Art Nouveau, the most accomplished artists set about acquiring a profound knowledge of plants, studying carefully their anatomy and structure. Steeped in these observations, they wedded them to design in inventive, imaginative ways. The results provided spectacular patterns for clothing, rugs, wall coverings, upholstery and other uses.

One group within the early Art Nouveau school embraced pale, light, pastel colors, using them for most of their work. Alphonse Mucha was perhaps the most notable exponent. As the movement matured, however, another group eschewed these faint colorations, replacing them with strong, bold hues. The work in this volume represents that tendency. As the first decade of the twentieth century progressed, the influence of Persian art and the Ballets Russes strengthened the domination of the colorists.

One of the most gifted designers in the first third of this century was E. A. Seguy. He produced numerous splendid albums that demonstrate the variety and abundance of his work. Viewing them, one marvels at the different transformations of his talent. Taken as a body they encompass the evolution of the decorative art of the period. The first collection, *Les fleurs et leurs applications décoratives,* was published in 1901 and is the subject of this book. It reveals how Seguy undertook the most exacting research to express the theories that were then in favor. For each of twenty flowers or pairs of flowers (thirty plants in all) Seguy would begin by using one plate for a literal depiction, often rendering the blossoms in several stages of development, from bud to mature blossom. In the following two plates he would interpret and apply these natural characteristics, transforming them into stylized design suggestions. Forty

plates showing 166 decorative patterns were thus conceived. All forty are contained in this book.

Many of these designs may be described as webby, lacy, airy, feathery and free. Often the floral pattern seems to grow of its own will, developing at leisure and spreading out along harmonious paths. The blue-petaled flower with green leaves on a mustard background in the lower left of the second Cineraria plate, the blue-green-veined and blue-budded flower with green leaves on a green field in the lower left of the second Lily plate, and the salmon-colored sweet pea with robin's-egg-blue leaves on a beige field in the upper right of the following plate are examples.

Other designs seem to be powered by supernatural energy and to grow rapidly within the confines of a small rectangular chamber, rushing pell-mell against the edges, distributing themselves with remarkably even proportions throughout. The orange and lavender arrowheads with green and rust leaves on a deep crimson background in the upper left of the first plate, the bunches of white flowers and green balls with flapping gray and green leaves on a gold background at the top of the second Cineraria plate, the spiraling white foxgloves with violet centers and orange leaves at the top of the following plate, and the royal-blue flowers with blue-green leaves on a blue-green field in the upper left of the second Rose Laurel plate suggest this type of development.

Other designs have an exaggerated upward bias, as if the flowers are responding to a magnet from above. Examples are the furling arums with the brown insides and lavender leaves at the upper right of the first plate, the royal-blue flowers with golden leaves on golden stems silhouetted in light blue-green on a deep blue-green field at the upper right of the first Buttercup plate, and the golden flowers with light brown stems and leaves on a mottled brown background at the upper left of the first Lily plate. A variation on the upward bias, in which the leaves show a somewhat horizontal as well as vertical tendency, is rendered in such marvelous designs as the lavender and rose hydrangeas with robin's-egg-blue and green leaves in the lower left of the first Celosia plate, the yellow flowers with brown leaves and green parts on a mottled yellow-green background at the lower left of the first Chrysanthemum plate, and the dusky blue flowers with green centers and brown leaves on a mottled brown field at the left center of the first Poppy plate.

Another favorite theme is the border entwined with flowers. Exceptionally beautiful examples are the yellow and white sunflowers with green leaves on a deep crimson and salmon field at the upper right of the first Foxglove plate, the deep crimson magnolias with light green and dark green leaves at the bottom of the second Magnolia plate, the crimson and white blooms with blue-green leaves on a deep salmon field at the top of the second Orchid plate, and the off-white flowers with deep purple stems on a mottled pearl background at the top of the second Rose plate.

Other designs are rendered complete for a household object, such as the rug on the second Chrysanthemum plate, the bookbinding and rug on the first Orchid plate, the dinner plates on the second Rose plate, the rug on the second Thistle plate, and the window on the first Water Lily plate.

The portfolio is an artistic and technical tour de force. The production method used was the pochoir process, a hand-coloring stencil technique employed to make many of the great design, fashion and architectural albums of the Art Nouveau and Art Deco periods. To accomplish the fine detail and shading, as many as twenty stencils were used to make a single plate. *Les fleurs et leurs applications décoratives* is distinguished by an exceptional watercolor-like freshness, in spite of its age of more than 75 years.

Having produced this first masterwork in 1901, E. A. Seguy continued his prodigious activity in Paris for the next 30 years, publishing *Textiles* (1910), *Primavera* (1913), *Floréal* (1914), *Samarkande* (1920), and, during the 1920s, *Insectes, Papillons, Les laques du Coromandel, Bouquets et frondaisons, Suggestions pour étoffes et tapis* and finally *Prismes* (1931).* His exceptional talent resulted in a dazzling artistic outpouring, one of the singular achievements of one of the great epochs of decorative art.

Washington, D. C.　　　Charles Rahn Fry

---

* The plates from *Bouquets et frondaisons* and *Suggestions pour étoffes et tapis* are combined in the Dover publication *Exotic Floral Patterns in Color* by E. A. Seguy. Nine plates from *Prismes* appear in Dover's *Art Deco Designs in Color*, edited by Charles Rahn Fry.

FULL-COLOR
FLORAL DESIGNS IN THE
ART NOUVEAU STYLE

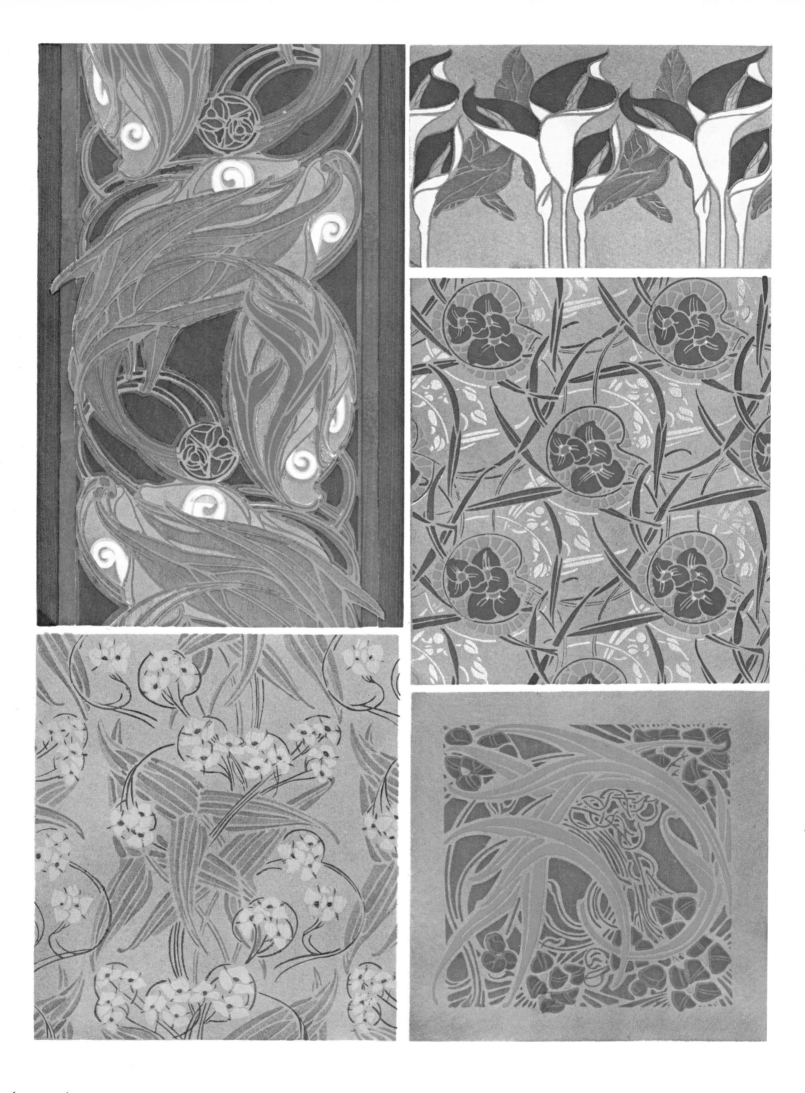

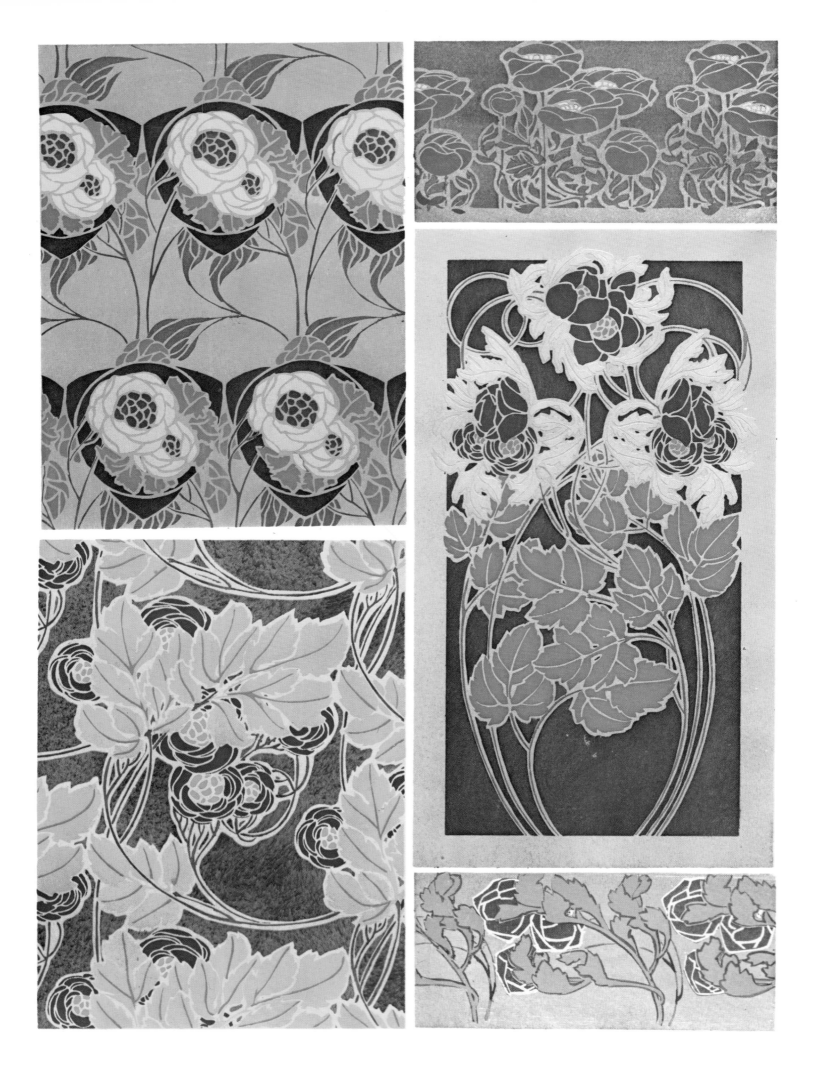

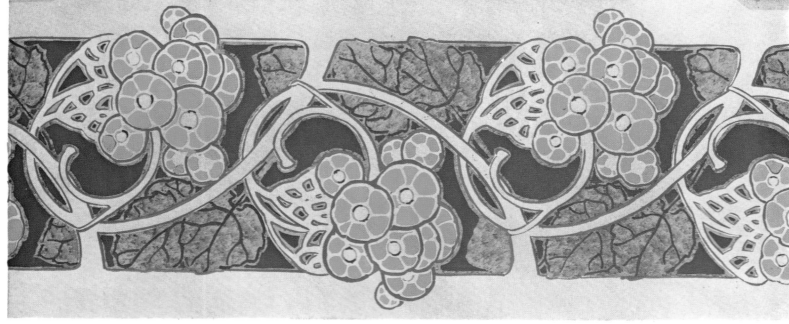

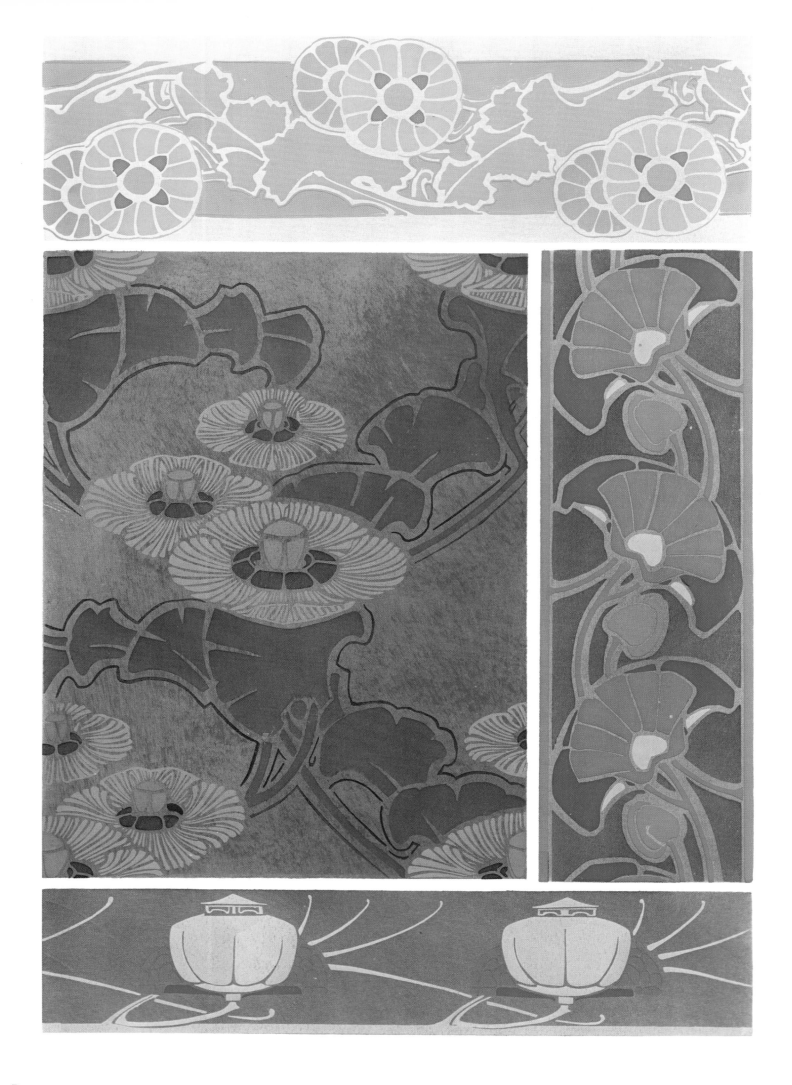

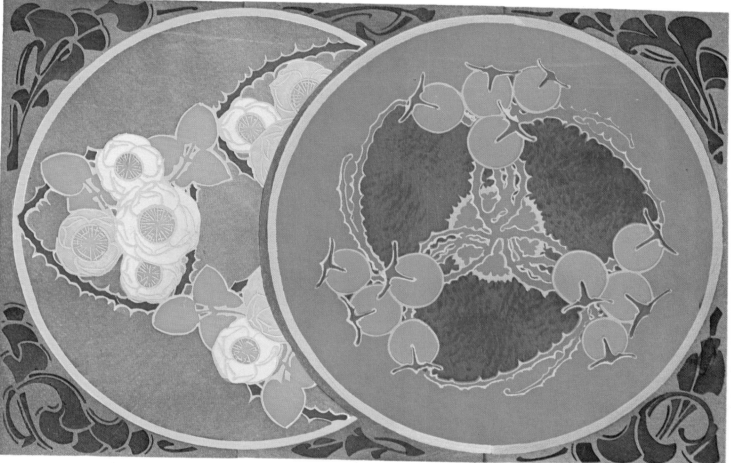

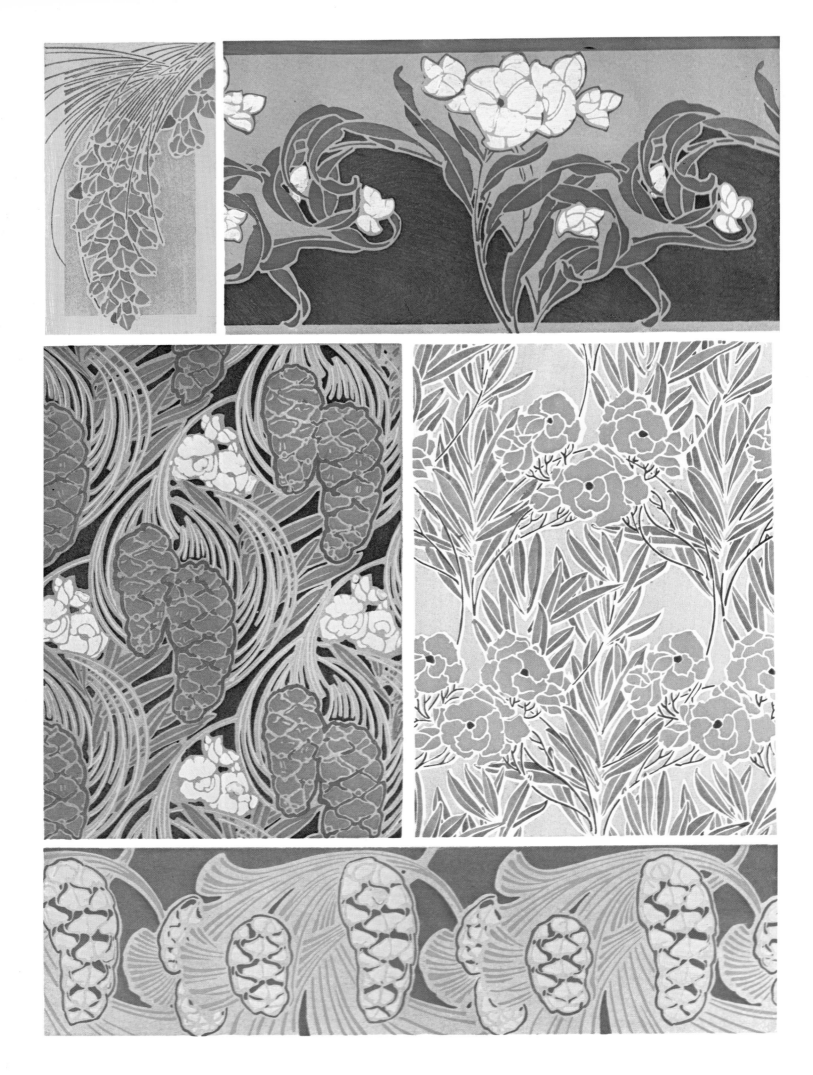

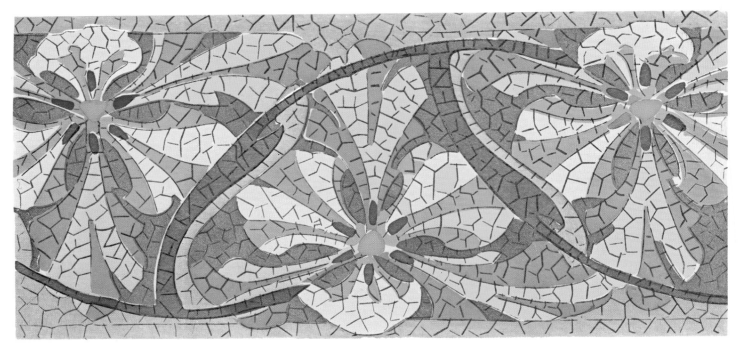